Family in Sixties

Alison Hurst

A & C Black · London

Black's Junior Reference Books
General Editor R J Unstead

2	Fish and the sea	25	Victorian children
3	Travel by road	26	Food and cooking
4	The story of aircraft	27	Wartime children
6	Mining coal	28	When the West was wild
8	Stars and space	29	Wash and brush up
9	Monasteries	30	Getting about in towns
10	Travel by sea	31	Canal people
12	Musical instruments	33	Home sweet home
14	Farming in Britain	34	Outdoor games
15	Law and order	35	Horses
16	Bicycles	36	Earthquakes and volcanoes
17	Heraldry	37	Going to school
18	Costume	38	The story of mathematics
21	Castles	39	Family in the Fifties
		40	Family in the Sixties

Hurst, Alison
 Family in the Sixties.–(Black's junior reference books)
 1. Great Britain–Social life and customs–1945– —Juvenile literature
 I. Title
 941.085'6   DA589.4

ISBN 0–7136–2704–2

Published by A & C Black (Publishers) Limited
35 Bedford Row, London WC1R 4JH

© 1987 A & C Black (Publishers) Limited
First published 1987

All rights reserved. No part of this publication may be reproduced, stored in a retrieval system, or transmitted, in any form or by any means, electronic, mechanical, photocopying, recording or otherwise, without prior permission in writing of A & C Black (Publishers) Limited.

Every effort has been made to trace and acknowledge copyright owners. If any right has been omitted, the publishers offer their apologies and will rectify this in subsequent editions following notification.

Typeset by August Filmsetting, Haydock, St Helens.
Printed in Great Britain by R J Acford Ltd, Chichester, Sussex

Contents

	Introduction	4
1	A prosperous decade	5
2	Education for all	16
3	Full employment	24
4	People on the move	33
5	The Swinging Sixties	39
6	Cinema and television	50
7	World events	55
	More books to read	61
	Some facts and figures from the 1960s	62
	Index	64

Introduction

Edward and Eileen Turner moved to Rustington Road, Oakley, at the end of the 1940s, with their baby son, John. Soon afterwards Sandra was born, and Angela followed in 1953.

At the beginning of the 1960s, all three Turner children were going to school. By the end of the 1960s both John and Sandra had left school and found jobs.

In 1964 Eileen took her first job since she married. In 1967, Edward was promoted and became a buyer at Kents, the department store where he had been employed all his working life.

These years are often known as the 'Swinging Sixties'. Dancing the 'Twist', ten pin bowling, Flower Power, the first Mini car and the first mini-skirts are just a few of the memories that some people – perhaps your parents – have of the 1960s.

In this book you can find out what life was like for the Turner family, living in Britain in the 1960s.

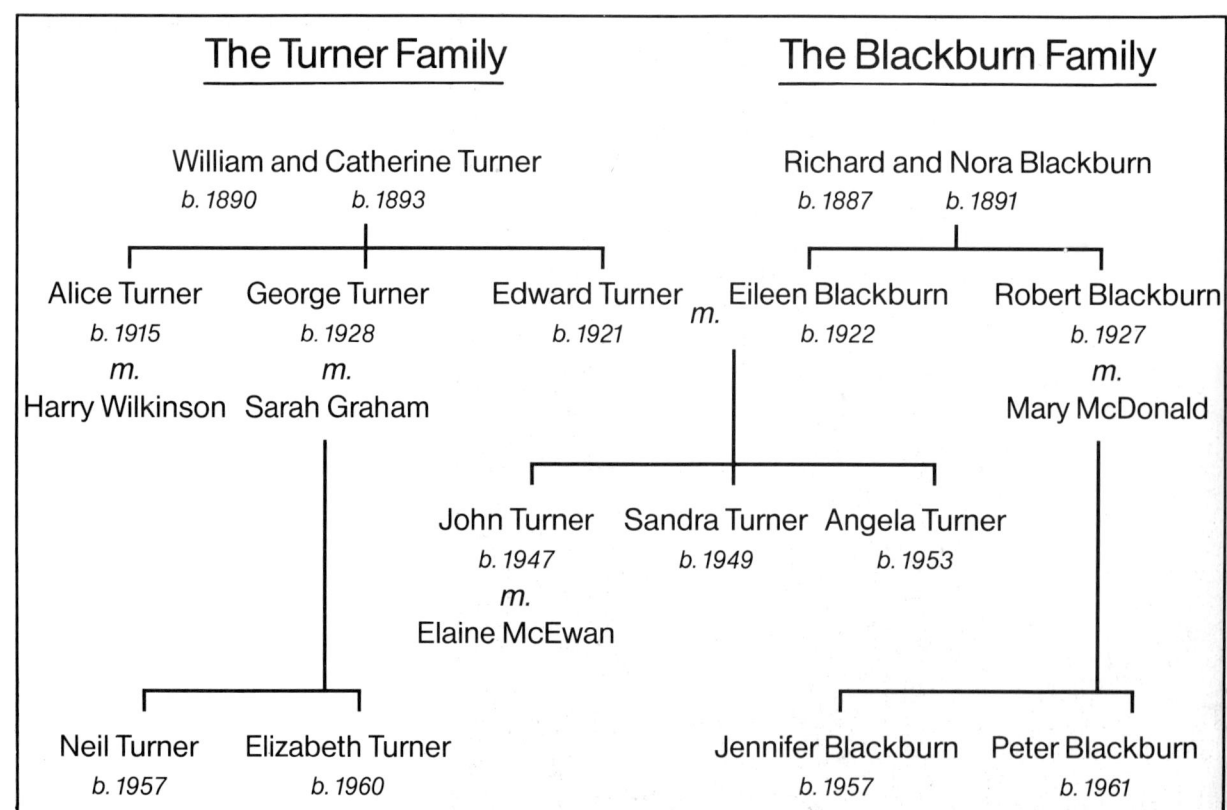

1   A prosperous decade

In 1959, the British Prime Minister, Harold Macmillan, had told the nation, 'You've never had it so good'. Five years later, in 1964, Labour won a General Election and Harold Wilson became Britain's youngest Prime Minister. Everyone looked forward to fresh ideas, new opportunities and a government that was in touch with the views of young people.

During the bleak post-war years many goods were still rationed and there was a lack of housing. But after some difficult years the nation looked forward to a brighter future.

By the 1960s Britain was prosperous. There were plenty of jobs and, although prices rose throughout these years, wages kept up with the cost of living.

Like many families in the 1960s, the Turners had more money and more leisure time than ever before.

Campaigning for change, 1965

Food and shopping

Edward Turner:
'There was a lot more variety in our lives than there had been for our parents. Even in everyday things, like food and groceries, there was more choice.'

There were new varieties of convenience foods that needed very little preparation. Almost every type of food could be bought in tins. Frozen 'Boil-in-the-bag' meals, complete dried packet meals and duo-cans were some of the new convenience foods.

John:
'I often had a pile of Smash and some fish-fingers when I came in from work, starving hungry and tired. Sometimes I'd mix a packet of Instant Whip for a quick pudding. Great stuff!'

Shoppers in a supermarket

Shops try to attract customers by offering more Green Shield stamps on certain days

New supermarkets opened up all over the country. For many people, shopping became a weekly instead of a daily excursion. Tesco, Safeway, Fine Fare, and many other stores became household names. Many of these supermarkets offered shopping 'stamps' as an incentive to buy more goods. Stamps were given according to how much you spent, and when you had collected enough stamps, you could exchange them for gifts chosen from a catalogue.

Eileen:
'I saved Green Shield and S & H pink stamps. There are quite a few things around the house which we bought with stamps – all our nice china and the ironing board and lots of other little things. Lots of people collected the stamps because it felt as though you were getting something for nothing.'

The stamps were so popular that shops had to try to out-do each other. Signs like 'Triple-stamps offered here!' were a common sight in shop windows.

An old ten shilling note

In 1966, plans for decimalized currency were introduced. Although the changeover from pounds, shillings and pence to 'new' money did not take place until 1971, some of the new coins were introduced in the 1960s.

Eileen:
'My mother was very upset when the old ten-shilling note was replaced with the 50 pence piece. She always called it ten shillings. Goodness knows what she would have thought about the £1 coin!'

The old-fashioned corner shops found it difficult to compete with the new supermarkets. Some corner shops began to stock different types of food which couldn't be bought in the supermarkets.

Eileen:
'When the Bhurjis took over the corner shop at the end of our road, they began to stock all kinds of fresh vegetables and spices that I'd never used before. Mr Bhurji didn't mind explaining how to prepare some of these. The children loved it when I cooked something different, but Edward still preferred his meat and two veg.'

Learning about the new currency at school

To compete with supermarkets, small shops stocked a wide variety of food. This butcher sells fruit and vegetables as well as meat

The Turners' house

There were other changes in the Turners' household. Edward and Eileen both became quite good at Do-It-Yourself decorating. More people were becoming interested in interior decoration, and magazines like *Homes and Gardens* and *Ideal Home* sold in great numbers.

One interior designer who became a well-known figure in the 1960s was David Hicks. He thought that people should build themselves a 'rumpus room', to be furnished with such items as a TV set 'covered in perspex so that you can see all the works'. Few of these ideas ever found their way into ordinary houses, but many people attempted to modernize their homes.

In 1964 Edward's younger brother, George, and his wife moved into a brand new house. The Turners loved to visit them in this ultra-modern style home.

Sandra:
'Uncle George's house was all open-plan design. There was no hall, so the stairs were in the lounge. The kitchen and dining room were designed as one room. There was a huge picture window and sliding doors leading into the garden. The whole house had a lovely feeling of space and light.'

A trendy TV set, covered with the names of various programmes

Kitchen interior of the 'Woman's Journal' House of the Year, 1961

Edward and Eileen had plenty of ideas about how they could modernize their own home.

Eileen:
'We replaced the kitchen table and cupboards with new kitchen units with formica tops, and put up venetian blinds in place of net curtains. Everything was in matching blue and white.'

The Turners bought some furniture in the modern style of the 1960s.

Edward:
'When we re-decorated our lounge, we had a fitted carpet put in for the first time. We got a really up-to-date three piece suite, made from the new vinyl material, and a long, low coffee table.'

In Sandra and Angela's room there were pop posters all over the walls.

Angela:
'We had a kidney-shaped dressing table with a pretty, gathered flounced trim round it, and matching curtains. Our bedspreads were made of quilted nylon and we had pink nylon sheets to match.'

John was lucky. He had his own bedroom.

John:
'It was great having my own room. I could take friends up there to play records and chat. One summer holiday, I covered a bedroom wall in paper that looked like pale wood.'

John and his sisters shared a portable Dansette record player. There were always arguments over whose turn it was to use it! John had the best collection of singles records, and he remembers paying 6s 8d (33p) for a single in the mid 1960s.

Spare time

The Turner family found they had enough spare time to take up new hobbies and interests. Like many other young people, John and his sisters used to visit the bowling alley.

Can you identify any of the stars on this wall?

Automatic record players became cheap and easily available

Down at the bowling alley

John:
'Suddenly, this was the "in" thing to do. I often went down to the local bowling alley with my friends Mike and Paul. We had to wear special soft shoes and we sat around drinking coke in between turns.'

The ten pin bowling craze came from the United States, and the first bowling alley opened in North London in 1960. Soon, many towns in Britain had bowling alleys.

Eileen and her friend, Jean Francis, joined Oakley Choral Society in the early 1960s. They found that their singing took up quite a lot of time, but at least they could practise at home! As well as choral societies, most large towns had amateur dramatic and operatic societies. The Turners' friends, Ron and Joyce Atkins, were keen members of the local operatic society.

At the weekend, Edward and his friend Ron played golf, a sport which was becoming increasingly popular. Golf tournaments were often shown on television. In 1969 Tony Jacklin became the first British golfer to win the British Open Championships for 18 years, and the following year he won the US Open.

John was more interested in football.

John:
'For the first time professional footballers could really make a lot of money – as well as being famous! In 1961 the player's maximum wage of £20 a week was abolished and in 1962 Johnny Haynes, the Fulham and England captain, became the first £100 a week footballer. It seemed like a fortune then. The best moment in English football for me was when Jeff Hurst scored the winning goal to beat West Germany in the 1966 World Cup Final.'

Social problems

There were some people, however, who didn't share in the general prosperity. As late as 1970, a survey showed that over $2\frac{1}{2}$ million people in Britain were still living in poverty. In 1965 there were more than 3 million people living in slum housing.

Slum housing in Liverpool, 1960

In many cities, high-rise flats were built as a quick and cheap solution to the housing problem. But these buildings often brought new problems.

Eileen:
'I remember when Ronan Point, a tower block in East London, collapsed – it filled the news headlines for ages. A gas explosion completely destroyed the building down one side and many people were killed. It was dreadful. People were terrified that high-rise buildings just weren't safe.'

Newspapers, radio and television all helped to make people aware of social problems outside their own neighbourhood.

Edward:
'Every time I opened a newspaper there seemed to be a new story about teenage crime. Eileen and I used to get worried when the children stayed out late, or we didn't know where they were. We read about the growing amount of juvenile delinquency in some areas and we just hoped they weren't mixing in bad company.

People realised that vandalism was often linked to poor social conditions

▲ Fetching the milk for Mum
◀ A sixties housing block

The Welfare State improved social conditions for many people. After the National Health Service was set up in 1948, diseases like typhoid and diphtheria, which had been mass killers, were virtually wiped out. More attention was given to the prevention of illness so there were more health visitors and people were encouraged to have vaccinations.

One of the most astonishing medical advances of the 1960s was the world's first heart transplant which was performed in 1967 by Dr Christian Barnard in South Africa. It was an historic operation reported by television and newspapers all over the world. The first transplant in Britain was carried out in 1968.

Doctors were becoming more concerned about the danger to health caused by smoking tobacco. A report by the Ministry of Health in 1969 showed that 100 000 people a year were dying from diseases connected with smoking. Previously, most people hadn't realised that smoking was connected with cancer and other illnesses.

Edward:
'I used to smoke about 20 cigarettes a day so I was horrified to read how many people in Britain were dying from lung cancer. It frightened me into breaking the habit – though it wasn't easy.'

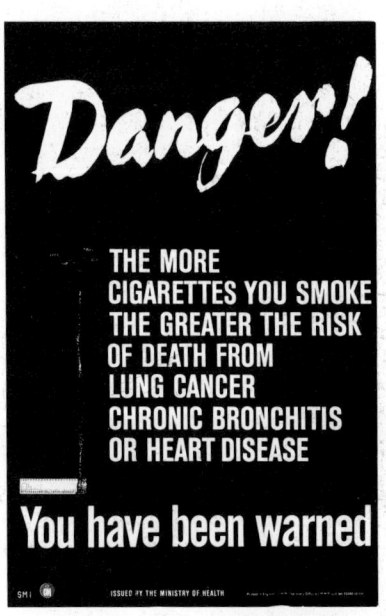

As early as 1962, warning signs against smoking were released

2 Education for all

Primary schools

In 1962, Angela's primary school moved into new buildings. Many of the old schools were becoming too small for the growing number of children starting school. Angela still remembers the excitement of having a new school to go to.

Angela:
'Everything was new and modern. There used to be old-fashioned blackboards on easels – now we had big green blackboards lining the walls. Instead of the double desks we'd shared before, we each had our own desks and chairs. But best of all there was so much more space to play in. The playground in our old school had been full of temporary classrooms.'

Victoria School, Islington in 1964

In those days, there was one set menu for lunch at school

Victoria School was rebuilt in 1968

17

The classroom had changed in other ways too. Teachers encouraged children to find out information for themselves and work in groups, rather than learning facts from the blackboard or by repeating what the teacher told them.

There was one change in school life which Angela remembers that nobody liked.

Angela:
'One of the things everyone liked to do was to ring the bell for the end of break. The headteacher used to choose someone to run around the playground ringing the bell. In the new school there was a buzzer to tell you when playtime was over.'

Children sitting their 11 Plus

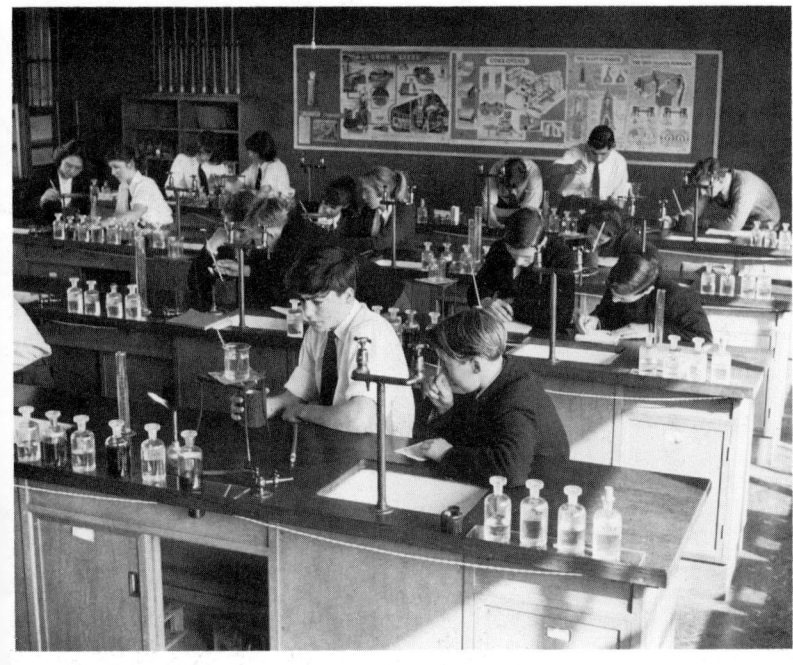

Science class at a grammar school

Comprehensive education

Until the 1960s, most children had to sit an exam called the 11 Plus in their last year at primary school. Those who passed went to grammar schools, and those who didn't went to secondary modern schools. Lots of people felt that this system was unfair. The different schools usually offered different opportunities to the pupils. In the grammar schools children were encouraged to take exams, but in most secondary modern schools the emphasis was on practical subjects that did not lead to GCE exams.

Many people were pleased when, in 1964, the Labour Government asked all local authorities to introduce comprehensive schools. The comprehensive system meant that everyone went to the same sort of secondary school, had the same opportunities to learn at their own pace and sit exams to suit their own abilities in each subject.

Edward:
'The comprehensive system seemed to me to be the only fair system possible. Some people protested about all the difficulties the changeover to comprehensive education would cause, but most people I knew were very happy about it.'

Sixth form girls

Angela in 1968

By the time the changeover to the comprehensive system happened, John and Sandra had already taken their 11 Plus. But Angela didn't have to sit the exam. In a large number of primary schools it was replaced with continuous assessment and regular tests. This meant that her primary school teachers made a note of her progress throughout the year.

By 1962 there were already 262 comprehensive schools. By 1970 the number of comprehensive schools had risen to 1 200. However, the changeover to the new system didn't always go smoothly.

John:
'My cousin Jennifer had two extra weeks holiday the year her area went comprehensive because the new school buildings hadn't been finished!'

Angela went to the new Moreton Comprehensive school. It was a massive school on a split site. One part of the school was in the old grammar school buildings and the other part of the old secondary modern.

Angela:
'I think there was a lot of confusion at first. Some teachers had to drive from one school to the other to teach lessons. But we all settled into a routine quickly enough.'

20

Boys learning to cook at a comprehensive

Kidbrooke – the first comprehensive

An important new exam, the CSE (Certificate of Secondary Education), was introduced into secondary schools in 1965. CSEs were designed to be taken at the same stage as GCE 'O' levels. This meant that far more pupils were taking exams at secondary school. Also, many more young people were deciding to go on to higher education.

Further education

New universities were opened all over the country and there was more choice in the subjects that could be studied at college or university. The new polytechnics offered many courses that trained students for particular sorts of work; for example, business studies, mechanical engineering or librarianship.

By the end of the 1960s there were over 300 000 students in higher education, twice as many as in the 1950s. This was still quite a small proportion of young people – the majority still left school at 15 to earn their own money.

When John left school in 1962, John's friend, Paul, decided to stay on to take some 'O' levels, which he needed to become an accountant. Paul worked hard; he passed in six subjects and was offered a job as an articled clerk with a local firm of accountants.

Girls learning to type at Ealing Technical College

Knees up at the local keep fit class

OPPORTUNITY — FOR YOU?
One-year residential course open to women over 20 interested in further education for personal enrichment or as opening to a new career. Subjects include LITERATURE, SOCIAL STUDIES, ECONOMICS, HISTORY, PSYCHOLOGY.
A chance to study and make new friends in pleasant college near London.
Non-political, undenominational.
GRANTS AVAILABLE.
Write NOW for prospectus and advice to
The Secretary (YW),
HILLCROFT COLLEGE, SURBITON, SURREY.

A course for further education is advertised in a YWCA bulletin, 1963

It wasn't just the young people who were benefiting from the education system. A great number of evening classes for adults were introduced, run by the WEA (Workers Educational Association) or local education authorities. Many older people, who had left school when they were very young, took advantage of the opportunity to study, or learn a new skill.

Adults who had left school unable to read or write had the chance to learn these skills at adult literacy classes. A lot of older people felt embarrassed about not being able to read or write and in the literacy classes they could learn alongside other people with similar difficulties. Many people were encouraged to go along to these classes, although it was not until the 1970s that a national campaign for literacy was mounted.

The Turners decided to enrol for some evening classes.

Edward:
'Eileen and I started off with badminton – to keep us in shape! Later on, Eileen took a course in French, and I spent a couple of years learning pottery.'

Eileen is sure that the confidence she gained from going to evening classes helped her greatly when she decided to begin work again.

By the end of the 1960s there were more opportunities for both children and adults to get the kind of education that suited them best.

Edward at his pottery class

3 Full employment

In 1964, when Angela began secondary school her mum, Eileen, took a part-time job in the offices of a local factory. She had not worked since before she married, and found many changes in office routine.

Eileen:
'I had never used photocopiers or an electric typewriter before. They made my job a lot easier.'

Offices were less formal. In the years before, calling people by their first names – 'Eileen' rather than 'Mrs Turner' would have sounded shockingly familiar, particularly if you were speaking to your boss.

Many employers were making an effort to make work surroundings more attractive and comfortable.

Eileen:
'I'm sure that people work more efficiently in pleasant surroundings. Where I worked, there were stylish new chairs and desks. Something else I appreciated – that I'd never seen at work in my young days – was lovely big pot-plants in the office.'

Women at work

Edward still worked for Kents, the department store where he had worked before the war. In 1967 he became a buyer for his department.

Edward:
'When they made me a buyer for the menswear department, I was very glad that I had teenage children about the house. A lot of the department stores were very slow to introduce some of the new men's fashions. I began to buy some of the more "with it" fashions as well as the standard menswear. Nothing too outrageous though – Kents wasn't that type of store.'

Edward enjoyed his job. His weekly wage was £24 11s 6d (£24.57), and in 1966 his annual paid holiday from work increased to 15 days a year.

Many people went on strike to try to improve their wages and working conditions. During the 1960s there were nearly 28 000 strikes in Britain – including stoppages by postmen, dustmen, teachers, bank clerks and seamen. In 1963 the Conservative Government tried to raise the general standard of working conditions. An Act of Parliament ordered that places of work should be clean, have good ventilation and lighting, that they should provide drinking water and washing facilities and be a comfortable temperature (not less than 60.8°F or 16°C).

Rubbish builds up during the dustmen's strike

Engineers' strike, March 1962

There were plenty of jobs available in the 1960s, though some of them were very monotonous. Manufacturing industries were using more automated processes to mass-produce identical items. Sometimes all that was left to do on the factory floor was to check that the product was perfect before packaging it.

Eileen:
'In the old days, there would be lots of people involved in manufacturing goods. Nowadays there seem to be more people in the office dealing with orders and bills and deliveries than actually making anything.'

Equal opportunities

In 1967, a man working in a factory was paid about £21 a week, but a woman was paid only £10 a week for doing the same work.

Sandra:
'I once worked as a packer in a crisps factory, putting packets of crisps into boxes. I was paid £6 10s (£6.50) a week and a lad who started the same time as me got £10. It did seem unfair!'

Making straw hats – small businesses, making their products by hand, found it hard to compete with increasing automation

Women on the assembly line at a greetings card factory

Throughout the 1960s, employers continued to offer low wages to women.

Eileen:
'I felt quite adventurous when I first went back to work. By the end of the 1960s, quite a number of friends, who also had grown-up families, had found jobs. Some of us regarded our pay as just pocket-money. But for youngsters like Sandra, it was the only income they had.'

In 1970, the Equal Pay Act was passed, so that 'the same work for the same pay' would be the rule.

It wasn't always easy to find a suitable job. A neighbour of the Turners', Sukhminder Bhurji, describes his experiences when he first arrived in this country. He was very disappointed not to be able to find a job that made use of his science degree.

Sukhminder:
'I was turned down for all the posts I applied for. It was quite usual then for employers to say 'No thanks, we don't want blacks here'. In the end, I had to take work on the night shift in a car factory, doing a very dirty job, for which I was paid very little – £12 a week.'

People protest against the 'colour' bill in Trafalgar Square, 1962. The bill imposed stricter regulations on immigration

Sukhminder had left the Punjab, in Northern India, in 1961. In that year 136 000 immigrants came to Britain. After the war, people, particularly from the Commonwealth countries, were encouraged to come to Britain as there were so many jobs available and not enough people to fill them. In the 1950s thousands of refugees from Europe came to Britain. The steady flow of immigrants from Africa, the Caribbean, Asia, Australia and Canada continued into the 1960s.

In many areas of Britain there was a lot of racism. When Nirmal Bhurji first came to Britain with her children to join her husband, she was shocked and upset by the way she was treated.

Nirmal:
'Sometimes I would walk along the street and a stranger would shout rude comments for no reason. It made me angry and unhappy, and I was afraid for the children going to school.'

In 1968, the Race Relations Act made it illegal to discriminate against anyone on the grounds of race or colour. However, it was often difficult to prove that you had been discriminated against.

By 1969 Sukhminder had saved enough money to buy a corner shop in Oakley, quite near the Turners' house, and the family moved into the flat above. Sukhminder still couldn't use his science degree, but at least he was his own boss.

Asian family in Rochdale

Starting work

When John left school at the age of 15, he had to decide what sort of job he wanted.

John:
'In those days there wasn't any worry about getting a job, as there was plenty of work about. When I was 14, I decided that the best thing to do would be to take an apprenticeship as an electrician. The pay when I started wasn't much – a first-year apprentice earned about £2 10s (£2.50) a week. This was less than Mike got for the job he had taken in a bakery (£4 a week).'

Youth employment officer talks to pupils at a secondary school

29

Young people studying for their exams at the local library

John didn't need 'O' levels to be accepted as an apprentice electrician, but he had to pass tests in both English and Maths when he was interviewed.

The new job meant many changes in his usual routine and it was sometimes difficult to find time to study.

John:
'In those days firms who employed apprentices didn't usually give time off for study. I had to work for my City and Guilds exams in the evenings and at weekends. When my apprenticeship finished and I'd passed my exams, I became an Approved Electrician and earned about £20 a week, which is more than most of my friends were paid in 1968.'

Sandra left school in 1965 with four 'O' levels. Her favourite subject at school was cookery, so she decided to try for a job where she could use this skill.

Sandra:
'I tried working in a cafe, but the most interesting thing they let me do was make ham sandwiches. I soon got fed up with this, and left.'

Over the next couple of years Sandra tried several different jobs, but she didn't feel happy with any of them. When she was 18, she decided to make a complete break, and find out what life was like in London.

Sandra:
'I know Mum and Dad were worried when I decided to leave home, and I'm sure they felt a bit hurt too. I just felt as if I needed a complete change, and I was determined to try living in London.'

When she arrived in London, Sandra found a room in a YWCA hostel. She took a job as a waitress in a coffee bar. The work was hard and at first she often felt very lonely – London seemed so big, busy and noisy. Luckily, Sandra soon became friendly with some girls in the hostel and began to enjoy life.

Sandra in London

The Alexandra Club – the first 'cluster' type hostel with bedrooms around a shared sitting room

A few months after Sandra arrived in London, she found a new home.

Sandra:

'I was offered a place in a house by some student friends. It was a great opportunity. The house was a crumbling old place in a road called Borneo Street. I shared a room with a girl called Marilyn but I didn't mind this. I was really pleased to be independent at last.'

Once Sandra was settled in Borneo Street, she found a new job. Her room-mate, Marilyn, worked at a health food restaurant called Crusts, and she suggested that Sandra went along to have a chat with the rest of the staff there, as extra help was needed. Sandra was really happy to start work at Crusts. The health food restaurant was a co-operative, which meant that all the men and women who worked there shared the different tasks, taking turns to buy the food, cook, clean and wait at table.

```
LONDON ACCOMMODATION
NEW YOUTH HOTEL IN WEST END
Hyde House, Bulstrode Street, London, W.1
140 beds for youth club and school journey
parties and individual bookings. Open all
the year round and 24 hours a day. 5 min-
utes walk from Bond Street and 10 minutes
from Oxford Circus.
Bed and Breakfast:
    Dormitory 12/6 a night.
    Single or double room (h. and c.) 17/6
Large lounge with piano and T.V. Pleasant dining
room. Evening snacks by arrangement. Central
heating and lift.
Baths, showers and washing cubicles. Drying and
laundry facilities. Shop and automatic vendors.
Tannoy system.
Apply: Receptionist, Y.W.C.A., Hyde House, Bul-
strode Street, W.1. Telephone: WELbeck 7887.
```

The coffee bar where Sandra worked for a while

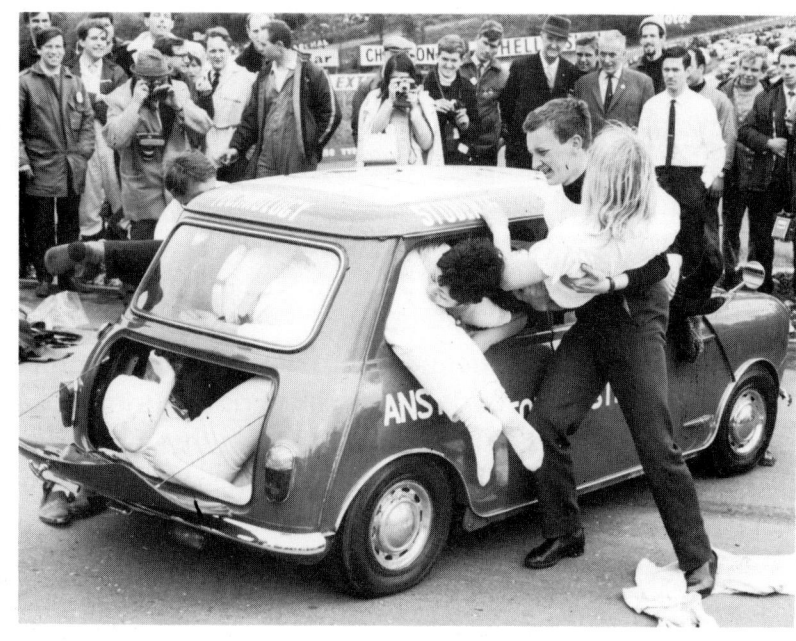

How many can you fit in a Mini?

4 People on the move

In 1964 Edward bought a green Mini – it cost him £425 plus £90 2s 1d (£90.10) tax. Eileen and all the Turner children learned to drive in this car.

Angela:
'It must have been a good model. It kept going with hardly any faults right up until 1975, and it certainly had a lot of use. I remember all of us, plus our luggage, packing into it when we went on holiday. Learning to drive it wasn't difficult, although you had to push a button on the floor to start the engine after you had switched the ignition on!'

The Mini was a best-seller right through the 1960s, and later.

There was a craze for cramming as many people as possible into a Mini – usually to raise money for charity. Many attempts were made at this stunt, often by students. Lots of different rules were used; sometimes the seats were taken out, sometimes children were included, sometimes arms and legs were sticking out. Because of all the confusion over rules no-one is now able to agree on what the actual record number of people to fit into a Mini was!

Travel by road and rail

In 1963, a government enquiry into British Railways, organized by Dr Beeching, led to the closure of about one-third of all railway lines (about 5000 miles) and 3000 stations.

British Railways changed its name to British Rail and introduced new carriages, without corridors or toilets, to be used on short routes.

The rail closures meant that there was a lot more heavy traffic on the roads and many people campaigned to stop lorries going through small towns and villages.

By the end of the 1960s there were nearly 15 million cars in Britain. Almost half of all families had a car, and some families had two. With so many cars, parking in towns became a problem – town councils had to build multi-story car parks to provide enough parking space. Yellow lines and parking meters became a familiar sight in streets.

The first part of the M1 from London to the north had been opened in 1959. By 1969, 622 miles of motorway had been constructed, and by-passes had been built to ease the terrible traffic jams in towns.

The front page of the Daily Mirror, 28 March 1963

What to look out for if you were speeding!

Some people suffered as a result of the by-passes being built, as councils put compulsory purchase orders on buildings which were in the way of the planned roads. This meant that people had to sell their houses to the council and move, whether they wanted to or not.

The number of people killed in road accidents increased, and thousands were seriously injured, because there were few regulations for road users.

Valerie Francis, who lived near the Turners, had a horrifying experience.

Valerie:

'I was a passenger in my boyfriend's car at the time. There were no laws about wearing seat-belts and his car didn't even have them fitted. At a cross-roads another car drove right into the back of us, and we were sent flying through the windscreen. We were both in hospital for ages. He lost an eye and I broke my nose badly and had terrible cuts on my face. I still have a scar on my forehead from this accident.'

To try and cut down on car accidents, the 70 mph speed limit was introduced in 1967. In the same year stiff penalties for drinking and driving came into force, and the breathalyser was introduced to help the police detect drunken drivers.

One of the first posters about the new breathalyser

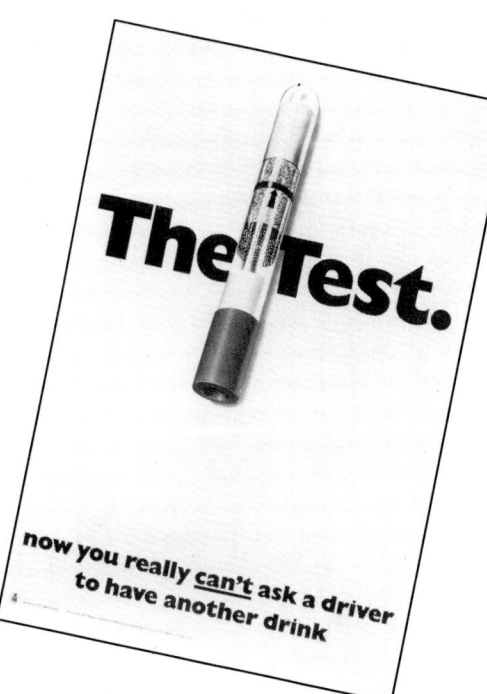

35

The RAC rally was a big event for enthusiasts in Britain

When John successfully completed his apprenticeship in 1968, he celebrated by buying a second-hand Ford Cortina, which cost him £200. With the Cortina he could do something he had dreamed about for ages - go on car rallies. The only problem was finding a navigator to sit in the passenger seat on these hair-raising journeys! His best friends were too busy to help him on a regular basis, and Angela gave up after her first attempt at navigating ended up with the car stuck up a muddy farm track followed by a furious argument between brother and sister!

In 1969 John met Elaine McEwan at a party.

John:
'Elaine and I liked each other straight away, and I soon discovered that she had an adventurous streak, as well as being very quick-witted. Before too long Elaine had become an expert navigator, and we had some marvellous times zooming round car rallies all over the place in the old Cortina!'

The 1960s ended on an exciting note for John and Elaine. They got engaged on New Year's Eve 1969.

Travel abroad

Travelling abroad became easier and cheaper during the 1960s. Fewer people took a traditional holiday in a hotel or boarding house at a British seaside resort. Instead many people decided to be more adventurous and go abroad on one of the new package tours.

John was the first of the Turners to go on holiday abroad. He went on a skiing trip to Switzerland when he was still at school. Later, he and his friends decided they'd like to go abroad somewhere else.

John:

'Mike, Paul and I wanted to go to Spain as it was the cheapest place to stay. The travel agent arranged everything for us. We travelled to Barcelona by coach, then caught a train to Sitges where we stayed. It was a real adventure for us, and it only cost £12 return by coach from London to Barcelona.'

100 perfectly planned HOLIDAYS in ITALY from 24 to 50 GNS. by Rail, Air, & Coach

Write to-day for FREE illustrated brochure: TRAVEL ITALY LTD. Dept. N6, 47 Beauchamp Place, London, S.W.3. Tel. Knightsbridge 424-

British schoolboys on a visit to Rome

Huntley & Palmer promote their biscuits with a competition for free holidays abroad

Package holidays organised by tour operators mean that more people could afford to fly abroad for their holidays. By the end of the 1960s gigantic jumbo jets could carry 500 passengers across the Atlantic in about 7 hours. Concorde 001, the first supersonic passenger aeroplane, made its maiden flight in 1969, but it was not until the 1970s that it went into regular service, flown by British Airways and Air France.

Another great achievement was in 1967 when Francis Chichester became the first person to sail single-handed around the world. He was 66 years old at the time and was knighted by the Queen for his achievement.

In 1962 a new way to travel was introduced. The hovercraft was invented during the 1950s by Christopher Cockerell, a boat builder from Suffolk. One of the first hovercraft ferry services was between Southsea and the Isle of Wight. By hovercraft, 30 people could make this 5 mile journey in 5 minutes. Soon there was a regular hovercraft service across the Channel.

Edward:
'We crossed the Channel in the first year of the hovercraft service. We had never travelled this way before, or visited France. I loved the sensation of 'hovering', but Eileen said it made her feel queasy.'

5 The Swinging Sixties

Fashion was fun in the 1960s, and for the first time fashionable clothes were available at prices young people could easily afford. Cathy McGowan, a TV personality from the pop programme *Ready Steady Go*, said 'The kids want clothes that look terrific – and they don't wear them for very long so it doesn't matter if they fall to bits!'. In the early Sixties a new word, 'boutique', began to be used for a small shop selling fashionable clothes.

Sandra:
'I used to meet my friends in the boutique in town every Saturday. It was the place to be seen. Even if we couldn't buy anything we tried on all the clothes!'

Most towns had at least a couple of boutiques by the late 1960s, but the centre of the boutique craze was Carnaby Street. During Sandra's first years in London, Carnaby Street was one of London's main tourist attractions. One weekend, Angela went to visit her sister.

Cathy McGowan and Tommy Quickly on *Ready Steady Go*

Boutique in Portobello Road, London

Angela:

'The boutiques in Carnaby Street were amazing! The walls were painted in psychedelic colours, and there were false archways and pillars all over the place. Of course, pop music was always playing in the background. I bought a pair of white plastic knee-length boots, and proudly took them home in a carrier bag with a Union Jack on it, and Carnaby Street written across the middle.'

Mary Quant and the new scene

The 1960s introduced outrageous and daring designs for clothes. Mary Quant is probably the best known fashion designer of the time. In 1962 the first colour supplement to a Sunday newspaper, *The Sunday Times*, was issued – the cover of this magazine showed a fashionable grey flannel dress designed by Mary Quant. The dress was modelled by Jean Shrimpton, and photographed by David Bailey. They were all part of the Chelsea group who were style-leaders and trend-setters of the 1960s.

Minis in a milk advertisement

School girls in their minis!

Covering up a mini with a maxi coat

In 1965 Mary Quant was described as the 'major fashion force in the world outside Paris'. This famous designer introduced the mini-skirt and tights, which replaced stockings and suspender belts. Most teenage girls of the 1960s wore mini-skirts.

Angela:
'When mini-skirts first came into fashion, we weren't sure we'd ever dare to wear them but soon we were cutting inches off our hems. At school, we used to turn our waist bands over to make our skirts really short.'

Twiggy was one of the most famous models of the 1960s. She was 'discovered' by Justin de Villeneuve who made her a household name.

Sandra:
'Twiggy made the "skinny look" fashionable. We all had to go on crash diets to slim down.'

The fashions of the Sixties were many, varied and sometimes confusing. Some of these strange styles included 'space-age' plastic clothing, throw-away paper dresses and floor-length 'maxi' coats for men and women. Most of the rules about what was suitable for different occasions were broken, and the bubbly, exciting ideas and original fashions of these years reflect the title of a hit song of the time – '*Anything goes*' (by the group Harper's Bizarre).

False eyelashes were carefully glued on, and taken off at night

In the early Sixties, fashionable men wore their hair short. Many favoured the 'mop top' look, made popular by the Beatles

Angela:
'I've always liked to wear trousers. When I was 10, stretchy ski-pants were fashionable. Towards the end of the sixties, when I was about 16, bell-bottomed jeans were the thing to wear.'

John:
'When I was 17 I got a suit with a round collar, which I was very proud of – it was the style the Beatles wore when they first became famous.'

Sandra:
'Heavy make-up, with false eyelashes and dark eye-liner, was very popular. At first, very pale lipstick was fashionable, but dark, plum shades became the favourites later in the 1960s.'

'Unisex' fashions

There were many different looks for hair. One of the most famous was the geometric style, worn by Mary Quant, which was short, straight and severe. It was a speciality of the hairdresser, Vidal Sassoon, another trend-setter of the time.

The Unisex look

When men started to grow their hair long there was a tremendous fuss. Most older people thought of these males as 'scruffy long-haired youths'.

John:
'My hair was only just over my collar, but Mum and Dad used to complain about it. We had a real battle when I wanted to grow sideboards. Mum never approved of these!'

The Unisex look began when girls began to wear denim jeans and jackets.

Angela:
'Some of the older generation used to complain that they couldn't tell which sex some of the young people were – they all wore trousers and had long hair!'

Beads and kaftans

In the later 1960s, many young people adopted the 'hippy' style of dress. Hippies were influenced by Eastern religions. They believed in peace, and that everyone should love one another. Their symbol was the flower and hippies became known as 'flower people'. Both men and women wore their hair in long, flowing locks, a fashion that soon caught on.

Sandra:

'I wore Kaftan dresses and strings of beads, or full, smock tops and long, flowing skirts. I had an Afghan coat with embroidery on it. The only trouble was that it used to smell awful; I think the goat skin it was made of had been only partly cured.'

Through all the varied styles of the Swinging Sixties, British dress designers stood out as world leaders in fashion.

Afghan coats were supposed to look scruffy and well worn

Pop music

Young people, in their teens and twenties, had an increasing amount of influence during the 1960s, as so many were able to earn a good wage. A lot of new entertainments were aimed at this age group, and many of the ideas came from this 'new generation'.

Most young people were interested in pop music. Listening to records, and to pop programmes on radio and television, going to pop concerts and discos – almost everyone under twenty was involved in 'the pop scene'.

There were tremendous changes in pop music during these years. Back in the 1950s, rock'n'roll had come from the United States and, until the early 1960s the USA dominated popular music. Then came the Beatles, who followed one hit record with another, made successful films, started off new fashions in clothes and haircuts and had millions of devoted fans throughout the world.

Sandra:
'I queued for two days and two nights to make sure of a good seat for a Beatles concert. When the concert began there was mass hysteria; we were so excited at the thought of actually seeing the Beatles that we went berserk. Once a few girls started screaming it seemed to affect all the others and we just lost control. Lots of girls had to be carried outside because they had fainted with excitement.'

The massive popularity of the Beatles was followed by great success for many other British groups. Suddenly, pop music charts all over the world were full of British records. The Rolling Stones, The Animals, The Searchers, The Who, The Kinks and many other groups from this country became international stars. Just about every week a new group emerged to become the latest pop music sensation.

The Charts, 6 January 1965

The Beatles at the end of the Sixties

Freddie and the Dreamers

Boy in a Derbyshire village

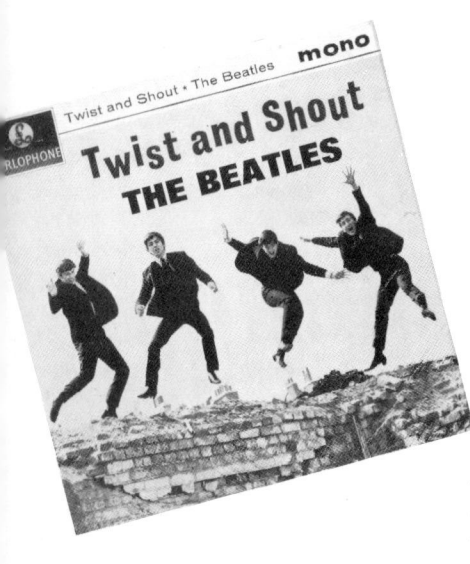

Record cover

There were hundreds of amateur pop groups. John began playing the guitar in a group when he was at school. After he left school, his group 'Zinc Stoat', continued to play together, and it was soon very much in demand locally, for school and youth club dances. Sandra and Angela felt really proud when their brother was up there on stage, playing at dances.

John:
'At school we had concentrated on rock'n'roll music. When we began playing for audiences, we tried to keep up with the music that was in the charts. We performed songs like *Twist and Shout, She loves you* and most of the Beatles' other hits. One of my favourites was *Ferry 'cross the Mersey*, a song recorded by Gerry and the Pacemakers. Sometimes we used to include classical guitar numbers – these usually went down very well.'

Sales of pop records grew and grew, as more young people bought record players. Luxembourg was still a favourite radio station with young people, but during the 1960s 'pirate' pop music stations began to broadcast without the crackly reception of Luxembourg.

Sandra:
'Radio Caroline, out in the North Sea, and other pirate stations like Radio Atlanta, played good pop music. In 1967 a law was passed which prevented these commercial stations from operating. I was sorry. Some of the DJs on these stations really made me laugh!'

Disc jockeys were a new sort of hero and many, like Alan Freeman and Tony Blackburn, became well-known household names. In 1967 the BBC created its own pop music station – Radio One.

The first discotheque opened in London in 1961. The atmosphere was different from that of a traditional dance hall. There was dancing to records played by a DJ, rather than to live music.

A new dance from New York, the Twist, soon took the place of the jive. You had to be very energetic to do the Twist for long.

Eileen:
'We didn't understand why the kids wanted to dance like that. It was so wild. You couldn't even tell who was dancing with whom.'

The Twist

Looking cool at a pop festival in London

Many pop stars, and other famous people of the time, were hippies. They became interested in Indian music and practised yoga and meditation. The Beatles' involvement with Transcendental Meditation under the guidance of an Indian mystic known as the Maharishi, led many people towards a search for 'inner peace'.

In August 1969 over 150 000 pop fans flocked to the Isle of Wight for the first major rock music festival in Britain. American rock stars, such as Bob Dylan, Jimmy Hendrix and Joni Mitchell played, as well as many famous British rock stars.

Sandra:
'It was an amazing experience! We camped out in the open for three days. The papers were full of stories about the terrible things that happened at pop festivals. Pop fans were accused of every crime from leaving litter all over the countryside to taking drugs. I thought this was rather unfair. On the Isle of Wight there was no trouble at all, as far as we could see.'

Classical music

Classical musicians like Pierre Boulez and Karlheinz Stockhausen explored new ways of making sounds into music. When Edward read about a piece the American composer John Cage had written he laughed:

Edward:
'It consisted of six radios, turned on together very loud all on different wavelengths. I couldn't believe that you could call this music.'

Theatre

In 1963, after many years of planning, the National Theatre was opened at the Old Vic in London. The following year Britain celebrated 400 years of Shakespeare.

In 1968 an Act of Parliament abolished the office of Lord Chamberlain, the official censor for the theatre. Before this, plays had to be carefully checked to make sure that nothing that could shock or offend the public (for example, acts of violence) was included. One of the first shows to take advantage of this new freedom was the musial *Hair*. Sandra went to this 'tribal, love-rock musical' with her boyfriend.

Sandra:
'I thought *Hair* was fantastic – quite different from anything I'd ever seen before. I must admit it gave me a bit of a shock at first to see naked people dancing about on stage!'

Cleo Laine and Jim Dale in a modern dress production of Midsummer Night's Dream at the Edinburgh Festival, 1967

Poster for A Hard Day's Night

6 Cinema and television

Andy Warhol, Pink Floyd and the Beatles were just some of the famous celebrities who became involved in films in the 1960s. Andy Warhol put many of his new ideas about art into his films. One of the more unusual films he made was a view of the Empire State Building during a working day. As you can imagine, not much happened on screen during the eight hours the film lasted! The band, Pink Floyd, used psychedelic films as a background to their concerts. The films were of very colourful, abstract shapes moving across the screen and added to the atmosphere of the music.

The Beatles' films were mostly comic musicals based on their songs. The films usually told a story, but they were very unlikely stories about spies and intrigue.

You might have seen some of the films made in the 1960s on television. *The Sound of Music* and *Mary Poppins* were both popular musicals and won Julie Andrews an Oscar film award. Sean Connery was an international success in the James Bond films.

Eileen:
'*Dr Zhivago* was one of the best films I've ever seen. It was a love story set in Russia at the time of the revolution, starring Omar Sharif and Julie Christie. I became so involved with the characters that I was quite exhausted when I left the cinema.'

John:
'I'll never forget going to see *2001: A Space Odyssey* in Leicester Square. I'd never seen anything like it. The sound track was in stereo and the screen was so big that you felt as though you were up there in space as well.'

The cinema was no longer as popular as it had been before television became a part of people's everyday lives. Between 1950 and 1970 the number of cinemas in Britain halved. When bingo became legal in the 1960s many of the closed-down cinemas were turned into bingo halls. The number of televisions increased every year. By the end of the 1960s, more than 9 out of 10 homes had a television.

The third television channel, BBC 2, was introduced in 1964 and, in 1967 colour television broadcasts began. Colour television was an expensive luxury for most people.

Edward:
'It was ages before we could afford to buy a colour television. In 1967 the cheapest colour television was £250 – that was the equivalent of about £1 250 now. Today you can buy one for less than £200!'

There were some memorable comedy programmes on television during these years, including *Steptoe and Son* and *Dad's Army*.

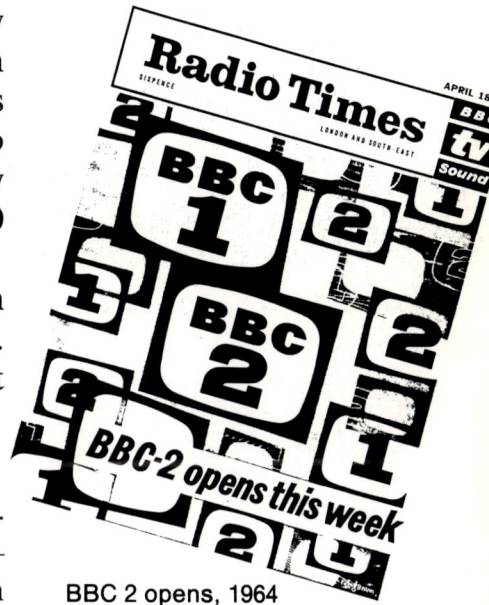

BBC 2 opens, 1964

Bingo and cinema all in one

John:
'My favourite was *Monty Python's Flying Circus* which was a series of manic comedy sketches and cartoons. I thought it was hilarious, but Mum and Dad couldn't see the humour. They would watch it for about five minutes and then walk out of the room shaking their heads, looking puzzled.'

Many television programmes of the 1960s are still running today, such as *Coronation Street, This is Your Life* and *Top of the Pops.* Of course, these programmes have had to change their style to keep up with the times.

Cilla Black, a pop star who first became famous in the Sixties

On the news

Television gave people the opportunity to share in the lives of famous people. The Royal family received a lot of TV coverage.

Eileen:
'It felt such a privilege to be able to watch Princess Margaret's wedding in 1960. And I must admit I shed a tear as though I was there myself. I watched the Prince of Wales' Investiture at Caernarvon Castle in 1969. The Queen conducted a ceremony in which Prince Charles was presented to the people of Wales on his 21st birthday.'

Television was not only a source of entertainment. Many people relied increasingly on the television for their news and information. The impact of live pictures often brought a sense of realism and urgency that newspapers couldn't match.

One of the dramatic news headlines was the Great Train Robbery in 1963. £2 580 000 was snatched from the Scotland–London Express.

John:
'The Great Train Robbery was talked about long after the event. The television cameras took you right to the scene of the crime where the police detectives were searching for evidence. I think a lot of people had a sneaking admiration for the gang. It took the police years to track down all the criminals. Today one of the robbers, Ronald Biggs, is quite famous, after escaping successfully and eventually seeking refuge in South America.'

An even more dramatic moment came in 1969 when the Americans succeeded in sending a space mission to the moon. The space race had begun in the late 1950s when the USSR launched the very first space satellites. This achievement was followed in 1961 by the news that the USSR had sent a man into space – Yuri Gagarin. Shortly after this, the United States managed to catch up by sending the astronauts Shepard and Glenn into orbit. But their crowning achievement was the Apollo XI space mission in 1969.

Prince Charles' Investiture at Caernarvon Castle, July 1969

People wait through the night to see the state funeral procession of Churchill

Angela:
'The whole idea of men in space seemed so far fetched until we saw it with our own eyes. We all stayed up until the early hours of the morning to watch the satellite pictures of Neil Armstrong walking on the moon's surface and planting the American flag. It was breathtaking.'

Television also brought less happy events into people's living rooms.

Edward:
'The state funeral of Sir Winston Churchill in 1965 was televised. Heads of State from all round the world attended. He had been an extraordinary wartime leader. John was given one of the commemorative coins they minted at the time.'

In 1966 a slag heap in the Welsh mining village of Aberfan collapsed, completely covering the village school. Almost 150 lives were lost, most of them children. Television coverage of this tragedy helped to prompt offers of help, messages of sympathy and donations from the general public, not only in Britain but around the world.

7 World events

John was sitting in his bedroom one evening with Mike, when they heard the news that caused one of the biggest shocks of the 1960s.

John:
'We were just chatting and listening to Radio Luxembourg, when suddenly the music was interrupted by a newsflash. We heard that the President of the United States, John F. Kennedy, had been assassinated. We just sat there, unable to take the news in. The pop music stopped; after a silence some serious music – it might have been the Death March – came on to the radio. President Kennedy had been a dynamic, young, forceful man. The idea of him being shot in cold blood shocked us. I think it must have been the first time an act of public violence had made a big impact on me. Mike and I sat there, shattered and sickened.'

In 1969, President Kennedy's brother, Senator Robert Kennedy, was also shot dead. Shortly after this, the world was horrified by the assassination of Martin Luther King, the American black leader and campaigner for Civil Rights (equal rights for all citizens).

In March 1963 (below), Kennedy was alive and well. In November he was shot dead on the streets of Dallas (above)

The Cuba crisis and CND

During the 1960s many events which shocked or horrified the world took place. The year John started work, 1962, was the year of the Cuba crisis. American spy planes found evidence that a nuclear missile base was being set up in Cuba, with the help of the USSR. The island of Cuba is just 160 km from the south-east coast of the United States, so the American navy immediately set up a blockade turning back Russian ships. The conflict over this made many people terrified that a nuclear war was about to break out.

John:
'There was a big sign daubed on the wall outside the place where I worked, with the words 'HANDS OFF CUBA'. Dad told me later that he, like many others, had been really frightened that World War Three had been about to break out.'

By the beginning of the 1960s the Campaign for Nuclear Disarmament (CND) had many members – in 1961 the annual CND march from the arms base at Aldermaston to London attracted 100 000 marchers.

Michael Foot and others on the Aldermaston CND march in 1960

Women protest against the mass slaughter of women and children in Vietnam

War in Vietnam

While she was going out with Andy, an American student, Sandra learned more about the war in Vietnam. In 1964 America had sent out great numbers of troops to try to prevent a Communist take-over of South Vietnam. People all over the world had different opinions as to whether America was right to become involved in this situation.

Sandra:
'Thousands of young people died in the Vietnamese war. I felt awful when Andy told me that a friend of his had lost his legs during the fighting. Whatever the politics were, it seemed wrong that all that bombing and bloodshed was taking place.'

Sandra's friends, Annie and Louise, who, like many university students, had been involved in anti-Vietnam protests, were interested to talk to Andy and hear about his experiences.

Queuing for a concert at the Roundhouse, London – a popular venue for modern theatre as well as music

Trying to put things right

During the late 1960s students were often in the news. 'Sit-ins' at colleges, organised marches, and protests about the way colleges and universities were run received a lot of publicity. Annie, studying at London University, felt that students did not deserve their bad reputation.

Annie:
'Some people seemed to think that all students were long-haired layabouts. We all worked very hard, and many of my friends worked for charity in addition to their studies.'

When she left university, Annie worked for the VSO (Voluntary Service Overseas). It was a way of helping people in developing countries, and offered the opportunity to experience life in a different part of the world.

There was, unhappily, a contrast between the vast amount of food available in the Western world and the starvation and suffering in some 'Third World' countries.

Angela:
'Sometimes I felt really guilty that I had so much to eat. We learnt about the dreadful living conditions in some of the Third World countries, at school. Television news and documentaries showed films of these miserable situations, and made many people realise for the first time that millions of human beings were dying from lack of food, water, or adequate medical care. A group of us from school organized fund-raising schemes for Oxfam, but we felt angry and helpless that there didn't seem to be much we could do to help.'

British people in the 1960s were keen to put coins into charity collection boxes. Charities like Oxfam, were particularly successful at this time, and many opened shops.

Young people were becoming more aware of the problems facing the environment, too. Air and sea pollution were giving causes for concern. In 1967 the 'Torrey Canyon', one of the massive new oil tankers, ran aground on the Cornish coast. Although no human lives were lost, thousands of seabirds had to be killed when their feathers became so saturated with oil that they could not fly. Eventually, the RAF had to be called in to bomb the tanker to prevent further oil leakage.

Oxfam appeal

In many ways the 1960s were disturbing years. Sandra tries to describe the mood of the decade as she remembers it.

Sandra:
'It was a time when we were made very aware, largely by newspapers and television, that there was an awful lot wrong with the world. Somehow, there was a feeling that now we knew what was wrong, we would be able to put it right. There was great hope for the future.'

In 1969 the voting age was lowered from 21 to 18. Angela was 16, and looked forward to having the vote in two years time. The young generation were excited at the prospect of having a say in the running of their country.

Young people at a festival in Hyde Park

More books to read

Growing up in the Swinging Sixties by Susan Cleeve (Wayland, 1980)
Growing up in the 1960s by Richard Tames (Batsford, 1983)

These story books were written in the 1960s and give a good idea of what life was like:
Jessica on her own by Mary K. Harris (Faber, 1978)
A dog so small by Philippa Pearce (Penguin, 1970)
Fly-by-night by K. M. Peyton (Sparrow, 1981)
Gumble's Yard by John Rowe Townsend (Viking Kestrel, 1984)

These books are for slightly older readers:
The Pendulum Years by Bernard Levin (Pan, 1972)
The Sixties by F. Wheen (Century, 1982)

Acknowledgements

AUTOCAR/QPL page 33
Barnaby's Picture Library pages 17 (top), 43, 47, 48
BBC Hulton Picture Library page 32 (bottom)
Coop pages 23 (top left), 24, 38
Crown copyright, permission of the Controller of HMSO page 35 (bottom)
Design Council Picture Library/Design Magazine page 9 (bottom)
Edinburgh International Festival page 49
John Frost Historical Newspaper Service 15 (bottom), 34, 51 (top), 55 (top)
Henry Grant pages 5, 6, 8 (bottom), 9 (top), 11 (top), 12, 13, 14, 15, (top left and right), 16, 17, (bottom), 18, 19, 20, 21, 22, 25 (bottom), 26, 27, 28, 29, 30, 37 (left), 39 (top), 41 (top), 42 (bottom), 44, 46, (top left and right), 50, 51 (bottom), 52, 56, 58, 60
LAT Photographic page 36
Melody Maker page 45 (top)
Metropolitan police page 35 (top)
National Dairy Council page 40
Oxfam page 59
Picturepoint Ltd – cover photo
Popperfoto pages 1, 3, 7, 11 (bottom), 25 (top), 39 (bottom), 41 (right), 42 (top), 45 (bottom), 53, 54, 55 (bottom), 57, 62, 63
Spink & Sons Ltd. page 8 (top)
Woman's Journal page 10
YWCA pages 23 (top right), 31, 32 (top)

Some facts and figures from the 1960s

Violet Carson and Pat Phoenix in Coronation Street, 1964

1960
Population of Great Britain about 46.3 million
3.5 million Britons take their holiday abroad
Campaign for British entry into the Common Market
John F. Kennedy elected President of the USA
Marriage of Princess Margaret
About 5.6 million private cars and vans in Britain
First episode of Coronation Street

1961
Average weekly earnings of man over 21 are £15 7s (£15.30)
USSR puts first man into space
The Times newspaper costs 5d (about 2p)
The large, white £5 note ceases to be legal tender
British Visitor's Passport introduced – valid one year, cost 7s 6d (37p)
London's first discotheque opens
'The Twist' dance becomes popular
Boy Scouts permitted to wear long trousers
Over 11 500 crimes of violence

1962
Cuba crisis
25 deaths from smallpox in Britain
First black Justice of the Peace appointed – in Nottingham
110 000 houses are damaged in Sheffield when gales rage over Britain
The Beatles' first single Love me do is released
Over one third of homes have refrigerators
World's first passenger hovercraft service – between Rhyl and Wallasey
262 comprehensive secondary schools in existence

1963
Unemployment reaches highest since war – 900 000
President Kennedy assassinated
Britain refused entry to Common Market
Test Ban Treaty (of atom bomb) signed by Britain, USA and USSR
USSR sends first woman into space – Valentina Tereshkova
Beatlemania sweeping the world
Great Train Robbery
Death of Pope John XXIII
Worst British winter for 200 years
Dr Who first appears on television
Dartford tunnel is opened
Summer Holiday film is released, starring Cliff Richard

1964
Harold Wilson becomes Prime Minister in Labour victory
Mods and Rockers riot
Tokyo Olympic Games – Mary Rand first British woman to win athletics gold medal (long jump) – Anne Packer first British woman to win track events gold medal (500 metres)
First Habitat shop opened
Mary Whitehouse sets up her 'Clean-up TV' campaign
BBC 2 broadcasts for the first time
The Sun newspaper launched

Alan Freeman (left) and Tony Blackburn

1965
Churchill dies
GLC set up
Cigarette advertisements on television banned
BP strikes oil in the North Sea
750th anniversary of the signing of the Magna Carta
Beatles awarded MBE
Early Bird (world's first commercial satellite) launched – first television programme using this satellite is broadcast to 24 countries on 2 May

1966
The Aberfan slag heap disaster
Discovery of large gas reserves in the North Sea
England football team wins the World Cup
4.2 million private telephones in homes
Severn Bridge opened
Sheila Scott becomes holder of round-the-world air-speed record (28 656 miles in 33 days 3 minutes)
Mini skirts the height of fashion
Forsyte Saga first shown on British television

Christian Barnard and his wife

1967
Milton Keynes designated a new town for 250 000 people
Francis Chichester sails round the world single-handed
Colour television starts on BBC 2
Student unrest widespread – LSE (London School of Economics) students 'sit-in' from 13–21 March
The Six Day War between Egypt and Israel
Beatles meet Maharishi
Hippies all the rage
BBC Radio One first broadcasts
QE2 launched
London Bridge up for sale

1968
US Senator Robert Kennedy assassinated
Martin Luther King assassinated
Vietnam peace talks begin
Richard Nixon becomes US President
Student rioting continues
Olympic Games in Mexico City
Over 21 000 crimes of violence
First two decimal coins issued – 5p and 10p
World's biggest hovercraft launched at Cowes
Ronan Point collapses – the danger of high rise blocks is brought to people's attention

1969
Population of Great Britain about 49.25 million
First man on the moon
Investiture of the Prince of Wales
British Concorde makes its first flight
Old halfpennies and halfcrowns cease to be legal tender
The new seven-sided 50p coin is introduced
About 15 million private cars and vans in Britain
Permanent abolition of the death penalty

Index

Aberfan disaster 54
Afghan coats 44

Bailey, David 40
Barnard, Christian 15, 63
BBC 2 51
Beatles 42, 45, 46
bedroom 10–11
Beeching Dr 34
Bhurji family 8, 27–28
bingo 51
Black, Cilla 52
Blackburn, Tony 47
boutique 39
bowling 11–12
breathalyser 35
British Rail 34

Cage, John 49
Carnaby St 39–40
cars 34–35
Chelsea set 40
Chichester, Francis 38
Churchill 54
cinema 50–51
classical music 49
CND 56
Concorde 38
CSE exam 22
Cuba crisis 56

Decimalization 8

Eleven Plus exam 18–20
equal opportunities 26–28
evening classes 23

fashion 39–44
Flower Power 43
food 6, 8, 31, 32
football 13
Freeman, Alan 47
further education 22–23

64

Gagarin, Yuri 53
golf 12
Great Train Robbery 53
Green Shield stamps 7

Hair 49
heart transplants 15
hippies 43, 44, 48
holidays 37–38
housing 13–14
hovercrafts 38

immigration 27–28
interior design 9–11, 24
Isle of Wight festival 48

Jacklin, Tony 12
jobs, 21, 24–27

Kaftans 43–44
Kennedy, John 55
Kents store 4, 25
Kidbrooke school 20
kitchen 10
King, Martin Luther 55

literacy classes 23
London 31–32, 39–40
lounge 10–11

Macmillan, Harold 5
Maharishi 48
make-up 42
maxi coats 41
McGowan, Cathy 39
mini skirt 41
Mini 33
motorways 34

National Health Service 15
National Theatre 49

O levels 19, 22, 30
offices 24
Oxfam 59

parking 34
Pink Floyd 50
pirate radio stations 46–4
pop music 44–48
Prince Charles 52–53

Race Relations Act 28
Radio One 47
rally cars 36
Ready Steady Go 39
Ronan Point 14
Royal Family 52

Sassoon, Vidal 42
schools
    primary 16–18
    secondary 19–22
Shakespeare 49
shops 6–8
slums 13
social problems 13–15
space travel 53–54
starting work 29–31
strikes 25

television 51–54, 59
theatre 49
Third World 58–59
Torrey Canyon 59
travelling abroad 37–38
Twiggy 41
Twist 47

unisex look 42–43

vaccinations 15
vandalism 14
Vietnam war 5, 57
voting system 60
VSO 58

Wilson, Harold 5
working conditions 24–2!
World Cup 13

YWCA 31